Volume 2

CHORDMASTER
Chord Theory for Keyboard

How to Understand Chords

A COMPREHENSIVE CHORD STUDY

For Beginning and Advanced Musicians

Copyright © 2009 by Michael Ellis
All rights reserved.

ISBN: 978-0-578-01231-5

Reproduction in whole or in part is not permitted
without permission of the author.

Published by Mike Ellis Music Instruction
Website: http://www.ellismusiclessons.com

This book is dedicated to my son, John, and Mr. Terrill Gardner, without whom it would never have been possible.

Table of Contents

Chapter 1 Let's Get Started 1-1
   Your First Test 1-4
Chapter 2 Scales Made Easy 2-1
   Understanding ALL Music Theory Depends on Your Knowledge of TWO Things 2-2
   Figuring Out the D Major Scale 2-3
   Figuring Out the E Major Scale 2-4
   The Natural Major Scales 2-6
   NUMBERS – The Secret to Music Theory 2-7
   Your Second Test 2-8
Chapter 3 Chords from Scales 3-1
   Your LAST Test 3-5
   Congratulations, You've Completed the Basics 3-6
Chapter 4 Advanced Chord Theory 4-1
   Minor Chords 4-1
   Seventh Chords 4-3
   Substitutions – suspended, flat 5, and augmented 4-6
   Additions – 6th and Major 7th 4-10
   Combination Titles 4-12
   Diminished and Half-Diminished 4-15
   Added Notes 4-16
   Inversions 4-17
Chapter 5 The CHORDMASTER REVIEW PAGES 5-1
   CHORDMASTER CHORD LIST 5-2
   OVER 5,592 POSSIBLE CHORDS! 5-6

Why CHORDMASTER?

To begin, the Chordmaster method was developed by a professional teacher with twelve years of experience. It was during these years that Michael Ellis found that the study of music and specifically the study of chords and their structure was not the nebulous, huge conglomeration of knowledge that most books would have a student believe. The fact is that chord names are the instructions needed to build the chord if you know the <u>terminology</u>. When you see a chord name in a book, you should instantly understand what notes to play. After you have read this instruction manual, you will be able to make <u>any</u> chord. If you play an instrument besides the keyboard, you will still understand the construction of <u>any</u> chord name you see. All you will need to know is the "major" form of the chord for your instrument, be it guitar, bass, flute, or any instrument, and the meanings of the symbols of instructions.

So, why CHORDMASTER? It is simply because there is no longer the need to memorize hundreds or thousands of chords. Learn to understand the language of chord names, the instructions they give, and you will be a master of chord construction, guaranteed. And the most important reason to use the CHORDMASTER <u>How to Understand Chords</u> manual, is that **if you can devote yourself to just 53 (fifty-three) pages of instruction, you will be able to make and understand over 5,592 chords!**

How to Proceed Through This Manual

There will be several sections to this manual, in order of the progression from notes to simple chords, to advanced chord theory. It is imperative that you initially go through the manual from start to finish, in order. Don't skip any pages and don't skip any of the question and answer pages. When you have finished, you will be able to locate the review pages and refresh what you have read in a concise form that will allow your knowledge to grow in steps toward your goal. At the end, there is a summary review page of all the chords. This summary will make sense to you if you have gone through all the preceding sections. **Caution:** Jumping to the summary page prematurely will only serve to confuse and retard your learning. Please, take it a step at a time. A Mr. Barrier once told my brother, "Life by the inch is a cinch, it's life by the yard that's hard."

Chapter 1 Let's Get Started

We must first make no assumptions in what you know or don't know. So, let's start at the beginning. When some musicians hear chord names like "G minor seventh augmented", they begin to wonder how they will ever memorize **all** the chords that can be made. Chord theory is a system of understanding **how** chords are made, so you **DON'T** have to **MEMORIZE** hundreds or thousands of chords.

If you start at the beginning, you should first ask, "What is a note?"

A **note** (or tone) is *any single sound* which is **pleasing** to the ear. Any key you press on the keyboard produces a **NOTE. OK? GOOD!**

How many different kinds of notes exist? Would you believe that **only twelve different kinds of notes exist**? That's right. Only twelve different kinds of notes exist. The notes repeat up and down the keyboard from the Middle C note near the center of the keyboard. Take a look at a section of the keyboard, below.

There are "NATURAL" notes - A, B, C, D, E, F, G, and "SHARP" notes - D# (D sharp) and "FLAT" notes - Eb (E flat). Each SHARP note is the next note ABOVE (in sound) the natural note. The FLAT note is one note BELOW the natural note.

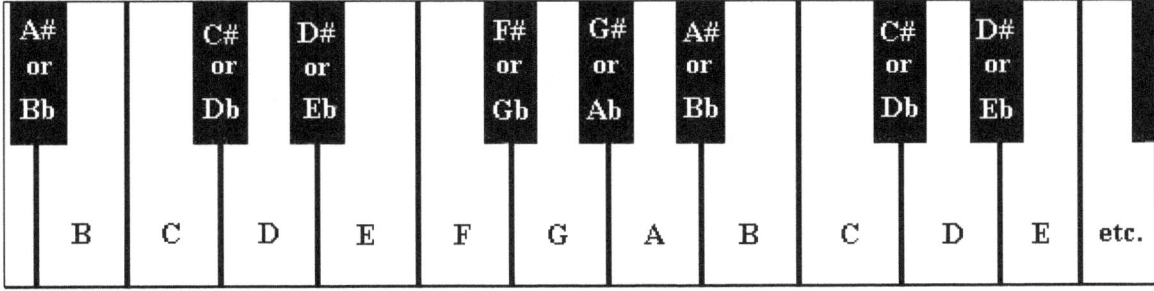

Figure 1

If you look at any of the black notes, above, they have two names with the word "or" between them. Because of this, A# can also be called Bb. There is a reason for this and it will be discussed later. For now, you can remember the sharp and flat names by remembering that you sharpen **up** a pencil, you sharpen **up** a knife, and you sharpen **up** your wits. You never sharpen anything down. You flatten things down. Another way to remember the names is that the sharp of one letter is also the flat of the next letter. The A# note is the Bb note. The sharp of the A note is the flat of the B note.

These black notes are actually sounds **between** the white notes. A better view of the keyboard is shown below. Remember that as the alphabet goes up, the sound of the notes also goes up. The C note is a higher "pitch" than the B note. You can hear this by playing them on your piano or keyboard.

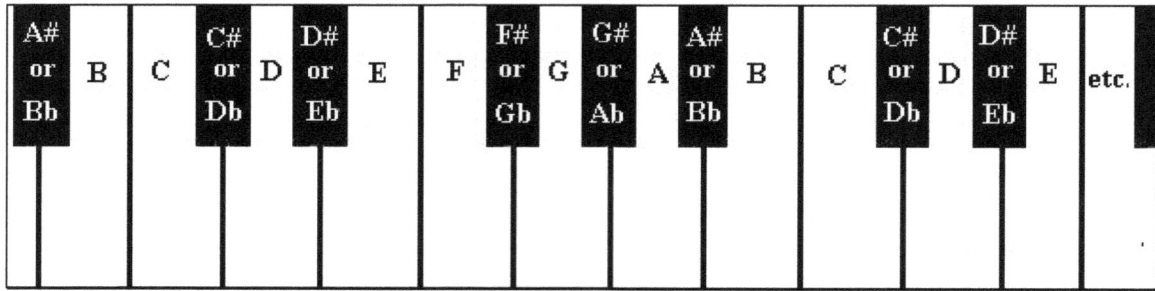

Figure 2

As said before, A# is Bb. C# is Db. Even though some notes have two names, there are still only 12 kinds of notes. If someone says "C", you have a concept of a C note, but you don't know which C they mean. How many C notes exist? That depends on what instrument you are using. Therefore, you can say that it does not matter, for now. You can have low C's, medium C's and high C's, but they are all just C's.

If we take a look at the notes in a chart format, it's really easy to see the order of the notes for further discussion. Notice that there is no note between B and C and there is no note between E and F in Figure 2 or Figure 3.

1	2	3	4	5	6	7	8	9	10	11	12	Repeat		
A	A# or Bb	B	C	C# or Db	D	D# or Eb	E	F	F# or Gb	G	G# or Ab	A	A# or Bb	B	C

→ up in sound →

Figure 3

Figure 1 shows the notes in alphabetical order and shows that they repeat after the G note. However, Figures 2 and 3 show the actual order of the notes and shows that they begin to repeat after the G# note. These pictures are very important for you to know and understand. Figure 3 shows the twelve notes in order and the direction of "pitch" by showing the "up in sound" direction marker at the bottom of the picture. You should already have experienced that playing the notes from left to right on a keyboard gives you higher and higher sounds. Now compare the picture above (Figure 3) to the second picture of the keyboard at the top of the page, Figure 2. Figure 3 starts the notes on "A" to show that the notes move alphabetically, A through G# (or Ab), and then they start over and repeat.

(It is necessary at this point to say that C is B#. That is because whenever you see a "#" sign, it means to move UP 1 note. So B# moves up 1 note from B. Since that note is C, then C could be called B#. F## is G, because the first "#" tells you to move UP 1 note from F to F# and the second "#" tells you to move UP 1 note again. Double sharps (##) are rare, and you should try to avoid them. Triple sharps are NEVER USED because F### would be just G#. Since you almost NEVER say B# for C or Cb for B, don't worry about those, yet.)

You READ note names and do what they tell you to do. For example, if you see G#, the G part of the name tells you to find a G note and then the "#" sign tells you to move UP 1 note. If you see a Db, the D part tells you to find a D note and then the "b" tells you to move DOWN 1 note.

Notes played in sequence make Melodies or Tunes. Notes played together make Chords.

Your main objective is to be able to make ANY chord whether you see the name in a songbook, hear somebody say it, or just want to make up one that you've never tried before. Along the way, you will pick up "Melodic" theory, which you can use to create songs or "moods" in your own music, and be able to better understand ALL music.

The most common type of chord is called the "major" chord. To make a major chord, just put your right thumb on the note that is the name of the chord you want to make, then count up four notes, not counting the one your thumb is on but including black notes, and play that note together with your thumb note, then count up three more notes and play that one together with the other two. For example, to play a C major chord, you play a C note with your right thumb, along with an E note and a G note. You can use any fingers you want to use to play the E and G notes. The E note is four notes up from the C note and the G note is three notes above the E note.

If you want to make a G chord, put your right thumb on a G note and count up four notes (which will give you the B note) and then three more notes (which will give you a D note) and play all three together. This is a G major chord. Most musicians and books call the C major chord the C chord and the G major chord the G chord, leaving out the word "major."

If you want to make an A chord, you play the A note with your right thumb and then play the C# note (up four notes from the A note) and the E note (up three more notes). So even if you need to use black notes, you always count up four notes and then three notes.

It's always the same for any major chord you want to play. Just count up four and three. Music really can be this easy. More about making chords will be discussed as you go through the manual, but it is a lot easier to understand chords and chord names if you understand major scales. These are discussed in the next chapter.

Your First Test

How many notes exist ? _____

What is the next note above C# ? _____

What is the next note below Ab ? _____

You should try to answer without going back to the previous pages, but if you need to do that, you can. The answers are at the bottom of this page, also. It's actually better to get the **right** answers than to guess and get the wrong answers.

Answers: 12, D, G.

Chapter 2 Scales Made Easy

When notes are played in sequence you get melodies or tunes. Three or more different kinds of notes played together make chords. If you only play two kinds of notes, it is called a simple harmony and not called a chord. Chords, harmonies, and melodies are created using notes from certain scales. The notes in a G chord come from the G MAJOR SCALE. For a C chord, the notes come from the C MAJOR SCALE. So what is a major scale?

A SCALE (major or any other type of musical scale) is a series of notes, which ascend and descend with a **SPECIFIC ORDER**. This means that EVERY TIME you make the notes sound going up, you always do it the SAME WAY. Likewise, when you go down, you always go down the same way. The MAJOR SCALE has a **SPECIFIC ORDER** to it. To move from the 1st scale note to the 2nd scale note, you must move UP 2 notes. This is called a "whole step". You can look at a scale on a "number line" to see what the ORDER is for major scales. Since the C MAJOR SCALE (or just the C scale) has NO sharps or flats in it, look at that scale before looking at any other major scales.

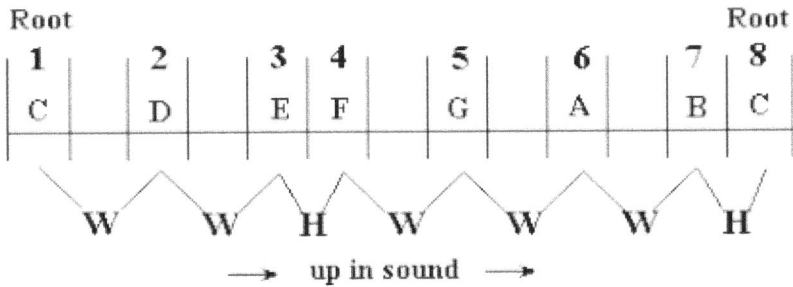

Figure 4

W = Whole step = up 2 notes   H = Half step = up 1 note

The most important part of Figure 4, above, is the steps shown below the horizontal line. The W's and H's are the **steps** that are taken in **every** major scale. It turns out that the C major scale has no sharps or flats. The reason for this is not really important and goes back ages. This is not a music history course. The fact remains that if you follow the steps shown in Figure 4, starting on any note, you will get the major scale for that note.

The "Set-up" for any major scale:

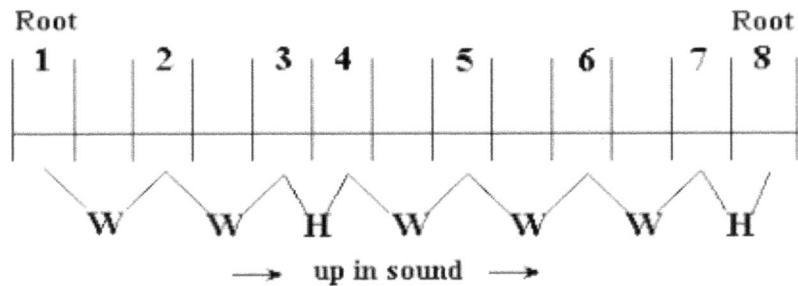

Figure 5

As said before, ALL major scales use this order. If you want to figure out ANY major scale, use the "SET-UP" shown above. From your first note, move UP 2 notes and you'll be on the 2nd scale note. Then move up 2 notes again and you'll be on the 3rd scale note. Then move UP 1 note for the HALF step and you'll be on the 4th scale note, etc.

Understanding ALL Music Theory Depends on Your Knowledge of TWO Things:

1. The **order** of ALL NOTES (A through G#) and

2. The **order** of MAJOR SCALES (the steps shown above).

These are the two most basic things that ALL music theory uses to derive Chords and Melodies. Memorize them!

So let's take a look at some of the other major scales. If we start on a D note, what notes will we get in the D major scale? First, write out the set-up.

Figure 6

If you always write out the set-up, first, you are less likely to make a mistake. ALL major scales ALWAYS move in ALPHABETICAL ORDER. You will NEVER see "C" and "C#" both in one major scale or see notes going "E" then "Gb". There is a "D" at the START and at the END of this scale. The first note and last note of EVERY major scale are the same KIND of note, called the ROOT. Now, you can do the D major scale.

Figuring Out the D Major Scale

```
Root         2         3    4         5         6         7    Root
 D  |    | E  |    | F# | G  |    | A  |    | B  |    |    |  D
 \___W___/ \___W___/ \_H_/ \___W___/ \___W___/ \___W___/ \_H_/
```
Figure 7

    A whole step UP from the Root or 1st scale note, D, will give you what note? **E.**

```
Root         2         3    4         5         6         7    Root
 D  |    | E  |    | F# |    |    |    |    |    |    |    |  D
 \___W___/ \___W___/ \_H_/ \___W___/ \___W___/ \___W___/ \_H_/
```
Figure 8

    A whole step UP from the 2nd scale note, E, will give you what note? **F#.**
(Remember the order of the notes on the keyboard.)

```
Root         2         3    4         5         6         7    Root
 D  |    | E  |    | F# | G  |    |    |    |    |    |    |  D
 \___W___/ \___W___/ \_H_/ \___W___/ \___W___/ \___W___/ \_H_/
```
Figure 9

    A half step UP from the 3rd scale note, F#, will give you what note? **G.**

```
Root         2         3    4         5         6         7    Root
 D  |    | E  |    | F# | G  |    | A  |    |    |    |    |  D
 \___W___/ \___W___/ \_H_/ \___W___/ \___W___/ \___W___/ \_H_/
```
Figure 10

    A whole step UP from the 4th scale note, G, will give you what note? **A.**

```
Root         2         3    4         5         6         7    Root
 D  |    | E  |    | F# | G  |    | A  |    | B  |    |    |  D
 \___W___/ \___W___/ \_H_/ \___W___/ \___W___/ \___W___/ \_H_/
```
Figure 11

    A whole step UP from the 5th scale note, A, will give you what note? **B.**

Figure 12

    A whole step UP from the 6th scale note, B, will give you what note? **C#. And you're finished.** The last step is done for you and can be used to check whether or not you made a mistake. If it really is a half step from your 7th note to the Root, then you probably wrote the scale correctly.

    Okay, let's take a look at another major scale. If we start on an E note, what notes will we get in the E major scale? First, write out the set-up.

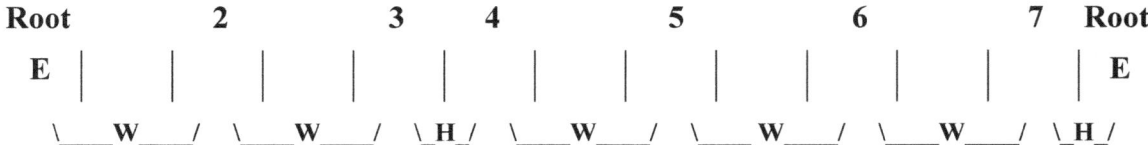

Figure 13

    If you always write out the set-up, first, you are less likely to make a mistake. ALL major scales ALWAYS move in ALPHABETICAL ORDER. You will NEVER see "C" and "C#" both in one major scale or see notes going "E" then "Gb". There is an "E" at the START and at the END of this scale. The first note and last note of EVERY major scale are the same KIND of note, called the ROOT. Now, you can do the E major scale.

Figuring Out the E Major Scale

Figure 14

    A whole step UP from the Root or 1st scale note, E, will give you what note? **F#.**

Figure 15

    A whole step UP from the 2nd scale note, F#, will give you what note? **G#. (Remember the order of notes.)**

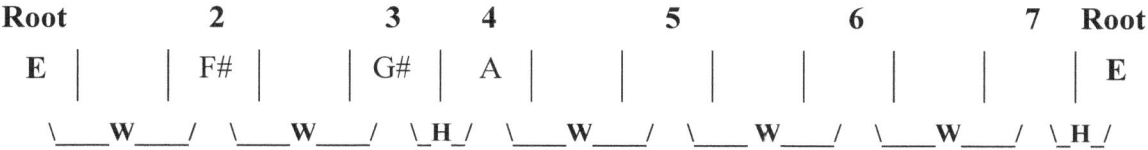

Figure 16

A half step UP from the 3rd scale note, G#, will give you what note? **A.**

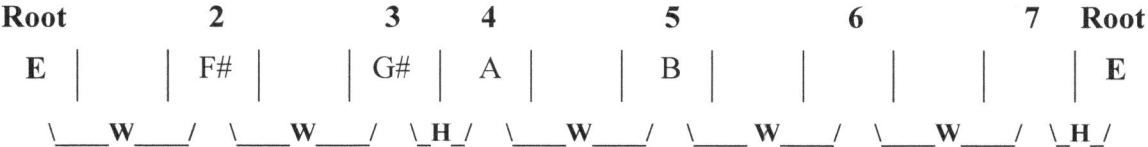

Figure 17

A whole step UP from the 4th scale note, A, will give you what note? **B.**

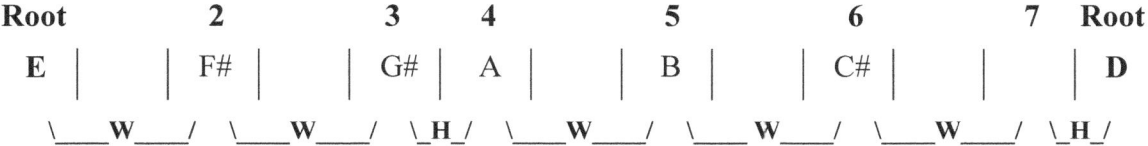

Figure 18

A whole step UP from the 5th scale note, B, will give you what note? **C#.**

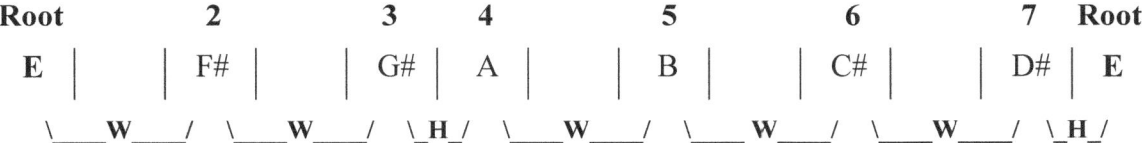

Figure 19

A whole step UP from the 6th scale note, C#, will give you what note? **D#. And you're finished.** The last step is done for you and can be used to check whether or not you made a mistake. If it really is a half step from your 7th note to the Root, then you probably wrote the scale correctly.

Notice: There are #'s in this scale. Every major scale except the C scale will have either #'s or b's in it.

Pull out some paper and try to do some for yourself. You can then use CHORDMASTER to check your work. The best way to get used to the order is to USE it. And you must know that **the ONLY HALF steps in ANY major scale are from note 3 to note 4 and from note 7 to note 8 (the Root).**

The Natural Major Scales

Here are the NATURAL major scales for you to **VIEW**.

R	2	3	4	5	6	7	R
A	B	C#	D	E	F#	G#	A
B	C#	D#	E	F#	G#	A#	B
C	D	E	F	G	A	B	C
D	E	F#	G	A	B	C#	D
E	F#	G#	A	B	C#	D#	E
F	G	A	Bb	C	D	E	F
G	A	B	C	D	E	F#	G
-W-	-W-	-H-	-W-	-W-	-W-	-H-	

Figure 20

Notice that it says "for you to **VIEW**" and **NOT** to **MEMORIZE**. The only two things you need to have memorized are the things mentioned before. They are: the **ORDER of ALL NOTES** and the **STEPS for any major scale**. If you know these two things, scales are easy to use. And now, if you are ready...

Look on the next page to learn the **SECRET OF MUSIC THEORY!**

NUMBERS – The Secret to Music Theory

That's right. NUMBERS. Music theory, or the discussion of concepts of music, must be done using numbers.

For example, all MAJOR CHORDS use only THREE KINDS of NOTES from the MAJOR SCALE, the 1st (or Root) note, the 3rd note, and the 5th note. The D major chord (you can just say the D chord) will use Roots, 3^{rds} and 5^{ths} from the D major scale. If you look at the Natural Major Scales, shown in Figure 20, at the D scale, you will see that the Root, 3rd, and 5th notes for a D chord are the D note, the F# note, and the A note. You can have as many of each kind as you like.

But hold on a minute... it said NUMBERS. That's right, because even though D contains D's, F#'s, and A's, the C chord contains C's, E's, and G's. An E chord contains E's, G#'s, and B's. Look it up! Do YOU want to MEMORIZE all of them? Nobody else wanted to either. If you stay in music long enough, you will end up memorizing them, but when musicians say MINOR, they mean that the 3rd scale note gets altered, regardless of whether it's the D minor chord or the C minor chord. It will always be the 3rd scale note and it gets lowered one note.

The letter name of that 3rd scale note is NOT what matters. What DOES matter is whether or not the player can FIND that 3rd scale note to alter it.

This is the heart of the next section - CHORDS.

Your Second Test

Please enter the steps below:

R ____ 2 ____ 3 ____ 4 ____ 5 ____ 6 ____ 7 ____ R
Your choices are: W-whole step   or   H-half step

How many different notes exist ? _____

What is the next note below F ? _____

What is the next note above B ? _____

Answers to Test 2:   W, W, H, W, W, W, H   and   12, E, C

Chapter 3 Chords from Scales

CONGRATULATIONS! You made it to the Chord section. As you saw on the last page of Chapter 2, Scales Made Easy, being able to find certain scale notes for chords will be the heart of this section. As a preface, you should know that once again memorization will be held to a minimum. However, it will still be necessary for you to have memorized the **STEPS** in all major scales and for you to know **the way all notes move** from A through G#.

A single sound is a NOTE. TWO notes (if different kinds) make what is called a SIMPLE HARMONY. CHORDS, however, are made up of THREE or MORE DIFFERENT KINDS of notes.

Two G notes plus one B note do NOT make a CHORD. The term DIFFERENT KINDS means exactly what it says. Even though a low G and a high G are different notes, they are the same KIND of notes... G notes. In an orchestra, if you have 15 violins and 7 play G notes, and 7 play D notes, and just 1 violin plays a B note, they've made a CHORD!

ALL CHORDS are DERIVED from MAJOR CHORDS. ALL MAJOR CHORDS use the MAJOR SCALE'S ROOTS, 3^{rds}, and 5^{ths}. MEMORIZE THIS!

To be able to locate the Roots, 3^{rds}, and 5^{ths}, you will need to know where they exist for your instrument. With CHORDMASTER, you will only be seeing the keyboard. But, since all notes will MOVE in the same order on ALL instruments, the information presented here will be helpful on ANY instrument.

Take a look at the keyboard again, on the next page.

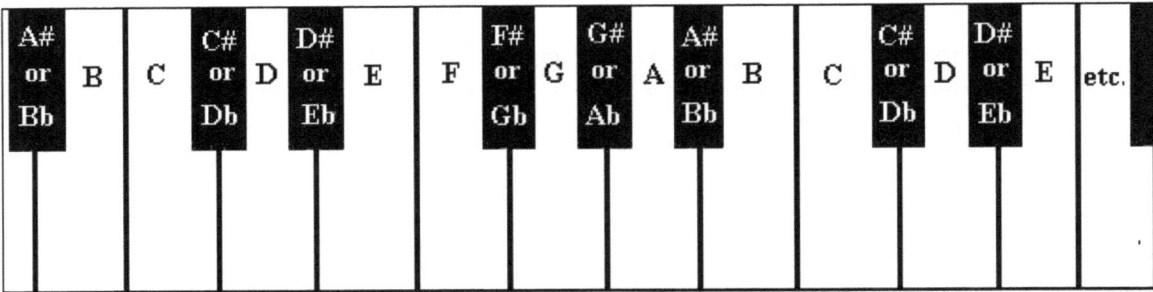

Figure 21

If you would want to make a simple C chord, you would first need to know where a C note is. If you want to make a complicated C chord like Cm7-5, you still need to know where a C note is, first. Remember, **ALL chords are DERIVED from MAJOR chords**. Going along this premise, look at some major chords on the keyboard.

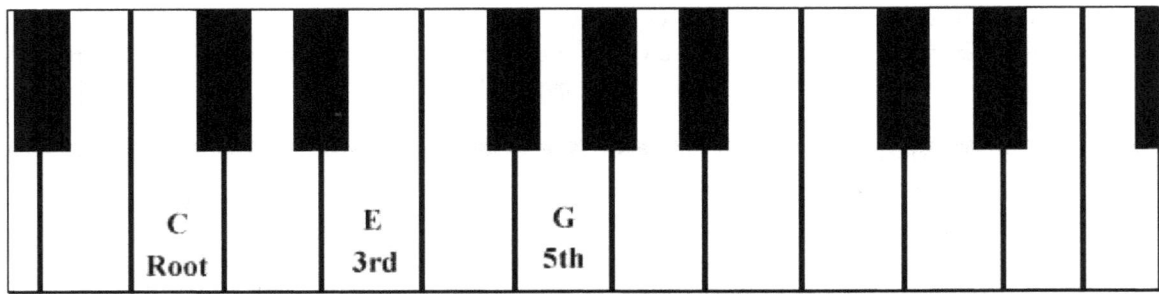

Figure 22

This is a C chord. You don't have to say C MAJOR CHORD, just C chord will do. The Root is on the C note. If you count UP from the Root note (not counting the Root note itself), you will see that from the Root to the 3rd is UP four notes. **Be sure to count the black notes, too!** From the 3rd to the 5th is UP three notes. Look at the Natural Major Scales on Page 2-6 to see that this is true.

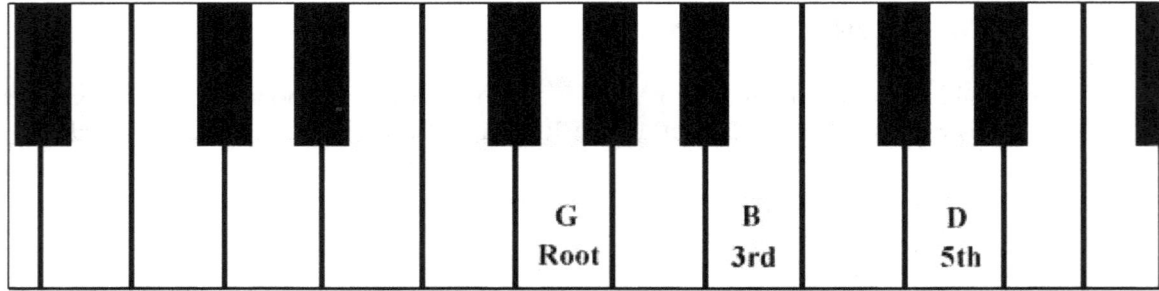

Figure 23

Here is a G chord. From the Root to the 3rd is UP 4 notes, again, and from the 3rd to the 5th is UP 3 notes, again. It will ALWAYS be that way. Remember the STEPS in a major scale? It is two Whole steps from the Root to the 3rd. That's four notes. Then, it is a Half step from the 3rd to the 4th and then it is a Whole step from the 4th to the 5th. That's three notes. The letter names on the 3rd and 5th in figures 22, 23, 24, and 25 are merely so you can look at the Natural Major Scales on Page 2-6 and verify that you are using the Root, 3rd, and 5th from the major scale for that chord. All you **really** need to know is the Root note name, and count up 4, then 3. It's that easy.

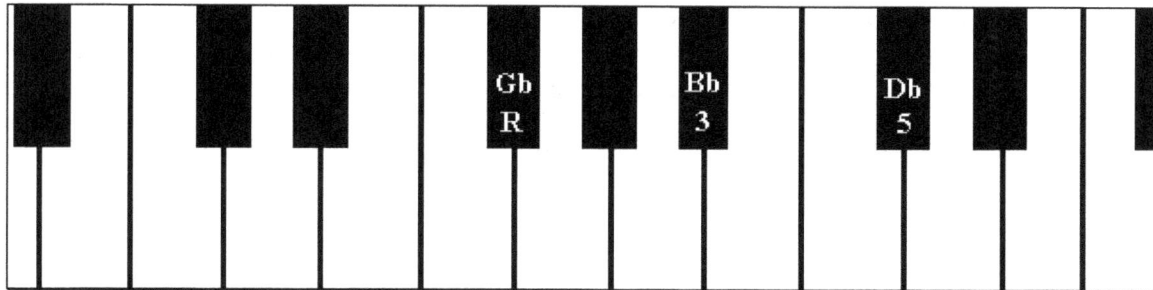

Figure 24

Here is Gb. The 3rd is still UP 4 notes from the Root and the 5th is still UP 3 notes from the 3rd.

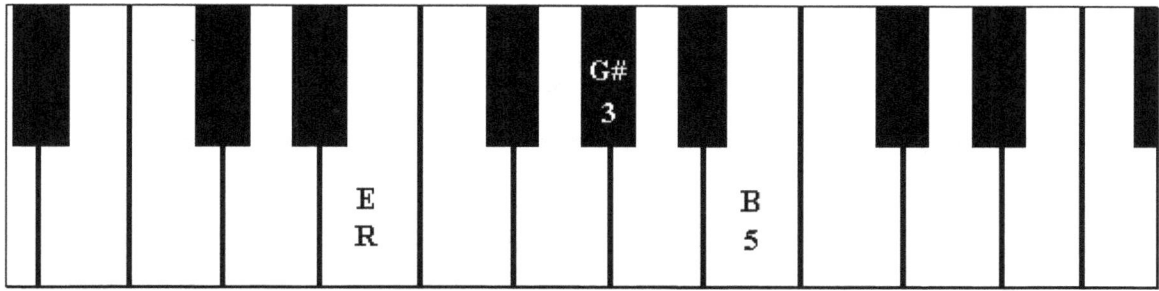

Figure 25

Here is E. The 3rd is still UP 4 notes from the Root and the 5th is still UP 3 notes from the 3rd. It's the same EVERY TIME.

So, regardless of the letter names of the 3rd and 5th, all you need to do is find the Root of the major chord you want to make, count up four notes, count up three notes, and play them together! It WILL BE the major chord for the Root you chose! Since there are twelve different notes, and all you have to do is follow the instructions just given, **you can now play ALL TWELVE MAJOR CHORDS! There are NO OTHERS. You can play ANY major chord in the world! You're GREAT!**

Find a piano... QUICK!

It is true that there are only twelve different kinds of notes, but if you look at the possible names of these notes, you can easily see that there are more than twelve names. If you consider the sharp and flat names, you get many more. Keeping the sharp and flat rules in mind (sharp means go up one note and flat means go down one note), how many different names would you find?

Most people would say there are seventeen. However, the fact that sharp means go up one note means that C could be called (and in some cases is called) B# and B could be called (and in some cases is called) Cb. The same holds true for E and F. The F note could be called E# and the E note could be called Fb. This would give you four more note names in addition to the seventeen, for a total of twenty-one actual possible note names. So you could say that you can play all twenty-one major chords.

In one book you might see a song with the Db chord used, while in another book you might see the C# chord used. If you know the way that the notes are named, you know that these two chords are just different names for the same chord and they will sound exactly the same. Therefore, this book will remain firm in the fact that there are really only twelve different kinds of notes and so there are only twelve different kinds of major chords. You will even be shown more than one way to make a major chord, but it will still be the same major chord, made by using a different location of the notes.

An example would be to make a C chord by using the E, G, and C notes instead of using the C, E, and G notes. It is the same three notes, just in a different order. But since it's still a C chord, you can still say that there really are only twelve different kinds of major chords. The rearranging of the notes will also be discussed more, later in the book.

Your LAST Test

Please answer the following questions:

What are the notes in any major chord? _____ , _____ , _____

Choices: R 2 3 4 5 6 7 R

How far is it...

from the 3rd scale note to the 4th scale note? _____

from the 4th scale note to the 5th scale note? _____
from the 1st scale note to the 2nd scale note? _____

Choices: W or H

Answers to your LAST test: R, 3, 5 and H, W, W

Congratulations, You've Completed the Basics

You have completed learning the basics needed to proceed to advanced chord theory. You should know by now that there is a sharp/flat between all the notes except B to C and E to F. You should know what a whole step is. You should know what a half step is. All of that is just the way notes move on any instrument.

You should know the order of the steps for the major scale. You should know that chords are made from notes in the major scale. You should be able to make (almost instantly) any of the twelve major chords.

That's quite a bit of knowledge, but that is just the start. From here you can go on to Advanced Chord Theory. Once again,

CONGRATULATIONS!

Chapter 4 Advanced Chord Theory

In this chapter, you will learn the language of Chord Names. Since these names are actually sets of instructions, you just read the instructions in the chord name and make the chord. You just need to remember that **all** chords are modifications or extensions of the **major** chord. You will always start with a major chord, and then follow the instructions given in the chord name. Since you can already play **every** major chord that exists, all you need to know is what the instructions are telling you. CHORDMASTER tells you in plain English, without any padding or fluff.

In all music, the most common chords are MAJOR chords, MINOR chords, and SEVENTH chords. If you know how to make these three basic kinds of chords, you are able to play MOST songs, in a basic form. It is worth mentioning that most POP songs are accompanied by chords. The keyboard player plays chords on many songs by playing the chord with the right hand and a single Root with the left hand. To begin advanced chord theory, you can say that you make chords other than major chords by either adding notes to the major chord or by substituting notes for existing notes within the major chord. It all starts with the major chord. You take a major chord and alter it or add to it (and often both).

Minor Chords

The first variation of the major chord is **MINOR**, the "sad" sound. This type of chord is made by using **substitution**. You use the **FLATTED 3rd** scale note **instead of the 3rd scale note**. Since ALL major chords use Roots, 3^{rds}, and 5^{ths}, then if the title of the chord has a lower-case "m", like "**Gm**" or "**Cm**", it will use Roots, Flatted 3^{rds}, and 5^{ths}. It is easier to say use R, 3b, and 5.

There can be as many of each note in the chord as you desire, but if the only title appearing after the chord's letter name is the "m", then the only change you need to make to the chord is to **substitute a flatted 3rd note for each 3rd note.** If you look at the Major Scale in Figure 26, you can see that there is a note in between the 2nd and 3rd scale notes. This note is called the FLATTED 3rd scale note. It is 1 note DOWN from the 3rd scale note, and **FLAT "b" means go DOWN 1 note**.

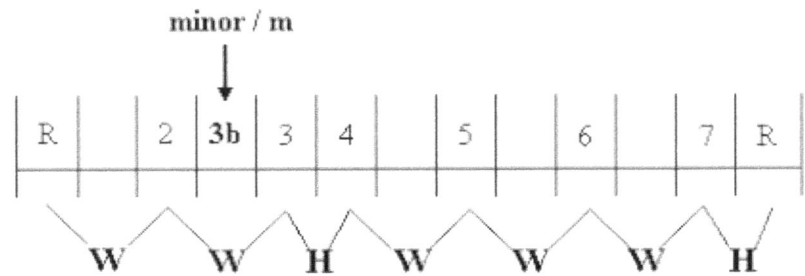

Figure 26

Don't memorize "R, 3b, 5" for MINOR. The "**m**" part of the chord name is always used to tell you to **substitute 3b for 3** in ANY chord. There is no such thing as a "minor family of chords" or a "group of minor chords" as some methods try to teach. You can take any chord and make its mood "sad" by flatting the 3rd scale note, making it **minor**. Minor simply means flat the 3rd scale note. Don't make it more complicated than it is. Just **flat the 3rd** whenever you see **"m"** in **any** chord name. You do have to be able to find the 3rd scale note, but that's easy, too!

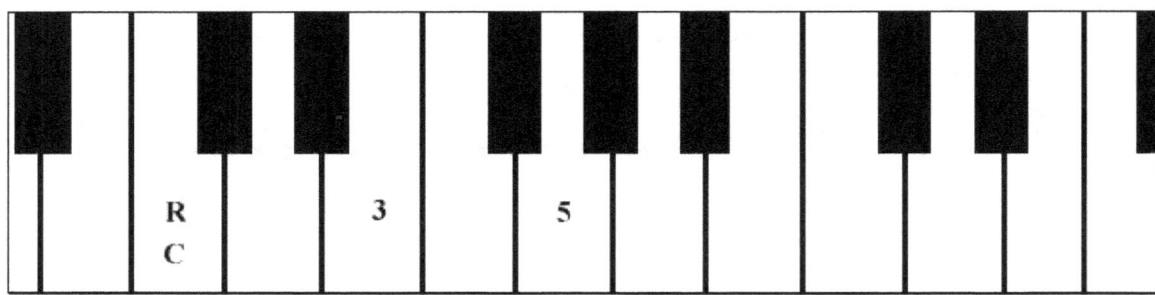

Figure 27

Above is a C chord. Below is a Cm chord. You call it a C minor chord.

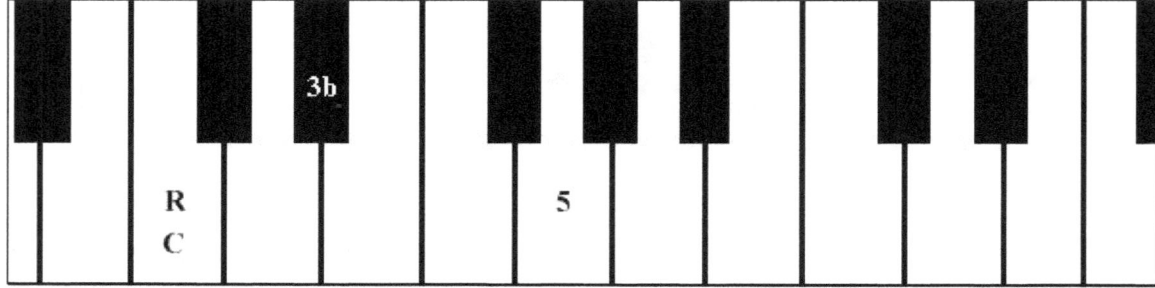

Figure 28

How easy can it get? You put in a **3b INSTEAD of a 3**. Now don't start counting how far it is between the notes shown above. The ONLY thing you need to remember about MINOR is to **use 3b instead of 3**.

How about an E chord and an Em chord?

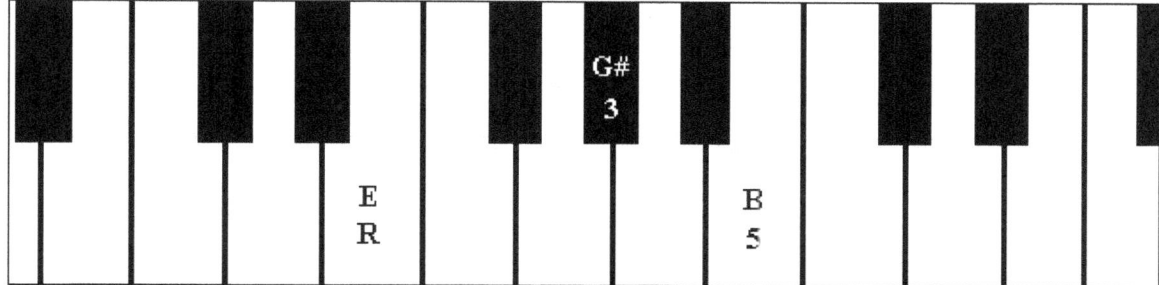

Figure 29

Above is an E chord. You found an E note, counted up four notes, counted up three notes and have the E chord. Now "m" tells you to lower the 3rd scale note. That's always the middle one of the three you have as the major chord. So now you lower the middle note one note, to the flatted 3rd for minor. Pretty simple.

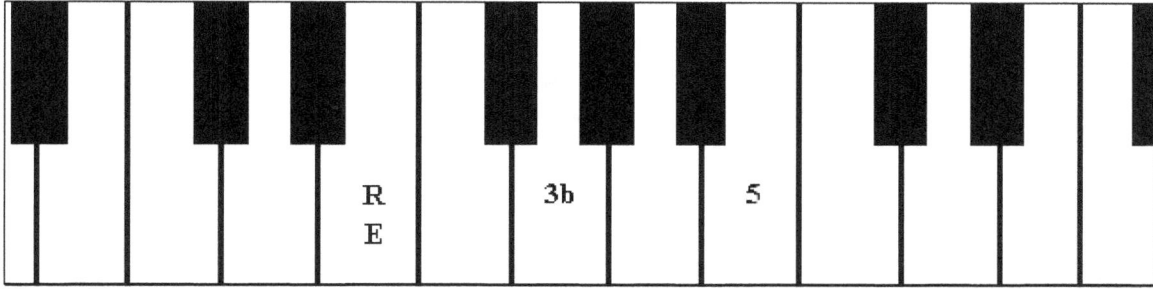

Figure 30

Here is an Em (E minor) chord, in Figure 30. Again, you use **3b instead of 3**. That's all you need to know about minor. Now, you can play **all twelve minor chords, too!**

Seventh Chords

Seventh chords (like D7) have a "pulling" sound. To hear it, play the chords G, D7, and G. Seventh chords are made by **adding a note** to an existing chord. If the title you see after the chord's letter name is "7", like "G7" or "F7", then you need to **ADD a 7b note** (FLATTED 7TH note). This note is found **2 notes below any Root note**. Look at figure 31, below.

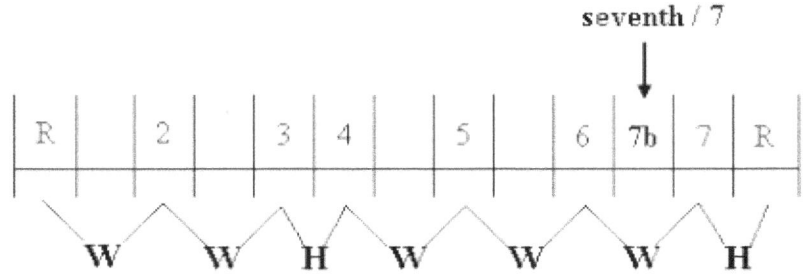

Figure 31

4-3

Discussion:

Why does the 7th chord use the **7b** note and **not just 7 note**? The real name of the 7th chord is "DOMINANT 7th". It is common practice to call it a 7th chord and leave off the word "Dominant." So you can say "G7" and not "G dominant 7th." The flatted 7th scale note is called the DOMINANT 7th note. Why is it called the dominant 7th scale note? It is probably because it is used more often than the 7th scale note. It dominates.

To make a 7th chord on the keyboard, you usually find a **Root**, above the 5th, and then go **DOWN 2 notes to the 7b note**. Add this note to the chord whenever you see the **7** in the chord name.

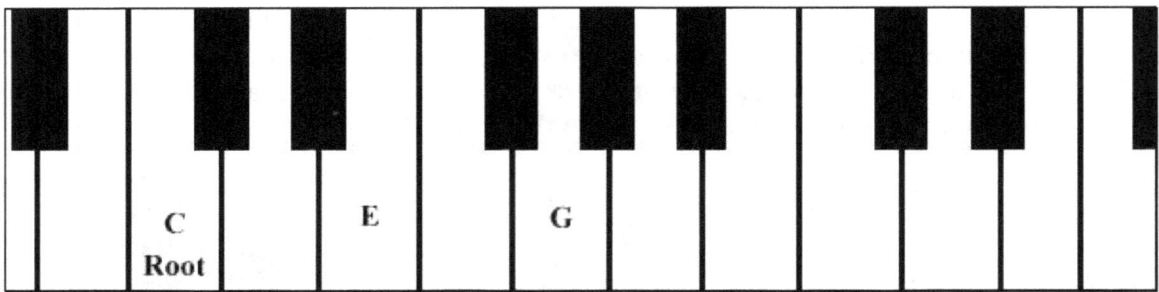
Figure 32

Figure 32 shows a C chord. A Root above the 5th shouldn't be hard to find, if you found the C Root in the first place. See below.

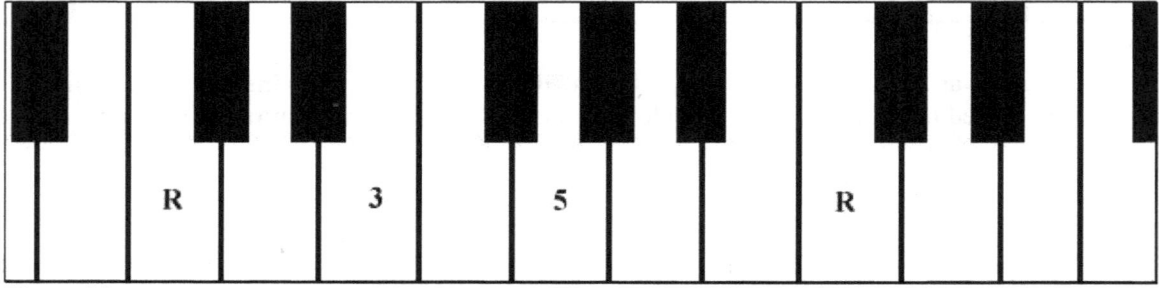
Figure 33

Figure 33 shows the C chord and the Root above the 5th scale note. If you move down two notes (counting the black note) to the 7b note and add it to the chord, you will have a C7 chord. This is usually said, "C seven" chord. See below.

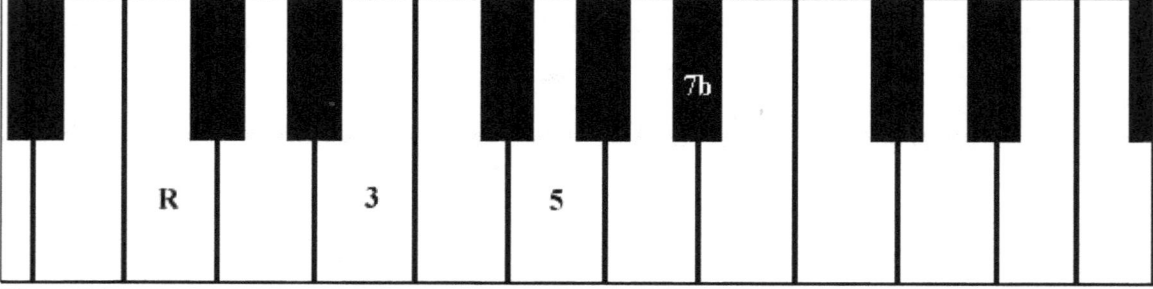
Figure 34

All you did was you **added a 7b note** to a C chord. By adding one note, you have a 7th chord.

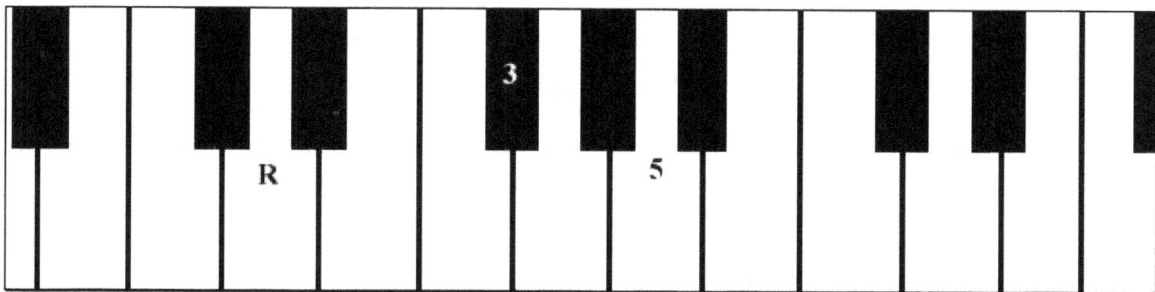
Figure 35

Figure 35 shows a D chord. Find a Root above the 5th, and then move DOWN 2 NOTES to the **7b** scale note.

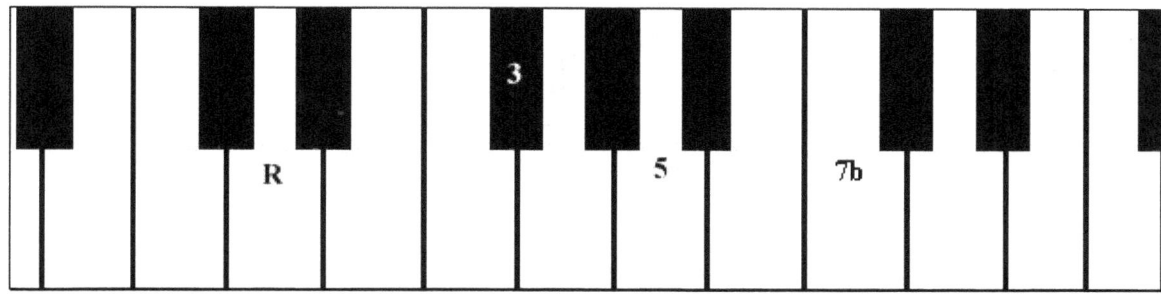
Figure 36

Figure 36 shows the D7 chord. The 7b is 2 notes below a Root, a D note in this case. The 7b chosen can be 2 notes below ANY Root. And remember, you can have as many of each note as you want to include in your chord. You can use two hands and have each one making a complete 7th chord. It's up to you HOW you make it sound, but it is most common to play the chord with the right hand and to play a Root in the bass with the left hand. Also, the most common version of the seventh chord is the one where you **find the Root** above the 5th and **MOVE DOWN 2 NOTES** to the **7b note** and add it to the chord.

A little recap is good. You know where the notes are on the keyboard so you can play **any major chord** by finding the name note of the chord and playing that note, the note 4 notes up, and the note 3 more notes up. That lets you play any of the 12 possible major chords.

Now if you can remember that minor (m) means flat the 3rd, you can play all 12 possible minor chords... **every minor chord that exists!**

And if you can find the Root and go down two notes to the 7b note, you can play all 12 possible seventh chords... **every 7th chord known to man!** WoW!

Substitutions – suspended, flat 5, and augmented

You have seen how minor uses the 3b scale note, instead of the 3rd scale note. This is an example of making a chord using **SUBSTITUTION**. There are three other examples of SUBSTITUTION. Each of these can be done within ANY chord. For example, you can take a G7-9 chord and make it minor, thus creating a G**m**7-9 chord by using the 3b instead of the 3rd. So regardless of the other pieces of title in the chord name, we **SUBSTITUTE 3b for 3 ANY TIME you see "m" in the name of a chord.**

The next example of substitution is SUSPENDED. When you see "**sus**" in a chord title, move **UP 1 note from the 3rd** and use that note instead of the 3rd. Look at Figure 37, below. One note UP from the 3rd is the 4th. However, if you think of it as **3#**, then you can say **the 3rd scale note can be FLATTED for MINOR or SHARPED for SUSPENDED.**

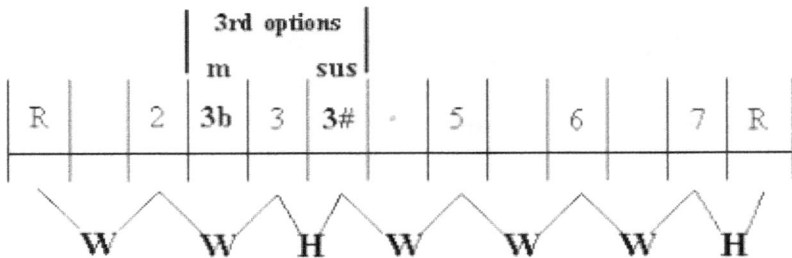

Figure 37

Notice that the "3b" in Figure 37, has "m" above it, for minor, and that the "3#" has "sus" above it, for suspended. The "3" has no title above it. **IF you DO NOT see "m" or "sus" in the title of a chord, you ALWAYS use the 3rd.** This is because ALL chords are derived from MAJOR (R,3,5). Therefore, if you don't see minor or suspended, then the chord's 3rd has not been altered. This is because no substitution for the 3rd scale note has been called for in the title of the chord. G**m**7 alters the 3rd, G7 doesn't.

On an earlier page, it was shown that you can make all 12 possible major chords. And you can make all 12 possible minor chords. And you can make all 12 possible 7th chords. This is all possible from knowing how to make a major chord and knowing **just two rules.**

Okay, a gold star to YOU, if you had ever heard of the minor seventh chord. Yes, to make a **minor seventh** chord, you make a major chord, **flat the 3rd for minor** and **add the 7b note for seventh** and you have the **m7** chord (like Gm7 or Cm7). By the way, that gives you 12 more chords! How easy is that?

Go to the next page for an evaluation of the chords you have learned.

Now add the possible chords for the all of the options given and look what you've learned.

12 major	12 minor	12 suspended	12 seventh	12 minor 7th	12 suspended 7th
	m	sus	7	m7	sus7
G	Gm	Gsus	G7	Gm7	Gsus7
Ab	Abm	Absus	Ab7	Abm7	Absus7
A	Am	Asus	A7	Am7	Asus7
B	Bm	Bsus	B7	Bm7	Bsus7
C	Cm	Csus	C7	Cm7	Csus7
etc.	etc.	etc.	etc.	etc.	etc.

That is literally <u>72 chords</u> from knowing <u>major</u> and <u>THREE RULES:</u> minor, 7th, and suspended. My... my... how MUCH you already know!

5th Scale Note Substitutions

The next example of substitution is **FLAT 5**. The 5th does not get used in an altered form very often. It usually just stays the 5th. But if it DOES get mentioned in the chord name, you need to know that it is a lot like the 3rd. It has a FLATTED option, which you call **flat 5** or **-5**.

Like the 3rd, the 5th has a sharp substitute as well as a flat. It is called AUGMENTED and is shown in chord titles by "**aug**" or "**+**". Most of the time, it is shown in chords with the "**+**" sign. **You use 5# instead of 5** when you see it anywhere in the title of a chord (G aug. or G+). See Figure 38, below.

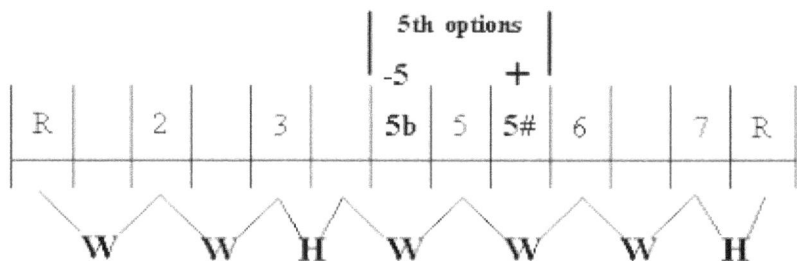

Figure 38

You can "Augment" ANY of the 72 chords on the previous page. That gives you another 72 chords. So now you know **144 chords**! You can also flat the 5th of ANY of them. That gives you another 72 chords. Add it up and you have **<u>216 chords from 5 rules</u>**! Try Dbm7-5 (Db minor 7th flat 5).

How much have you been required to **memorize** to know how to make **216 chords**?

First, there are the basics:

Where the notes are on the keyboard.
The **steps** for ANY major scale.
Major uses only Roots, 3^{rds}, and 5^{ths}. (Find the name note, count up 4, then 3.)

Then the five rules, so far:

Rule 1 - **minor** uses **3b** instead of the 3rd note.
Rule 2 - **seventh adds a 7b** note (2 notes below a Root).
Rule 3 - **suspended** uses **3#** instead the 3rd note.
Rule 4 - **flat 5** uses **5b** instead of the 5th note.
Rule 5 - **augmented** uses **5#** instead of the 5th note.

That's not quite like trying to memorize the 216 hand shapes from *pictures* in a chord book! Now look at them grouped.

ALWAYS START WITH MAJOR = R, 3, 5

3rd	minor / **m**	Use **3b**	instead of 3	**3b**
	suspended / **sus**	Use **3#** (4)	instead of 3	**3#**
5th	flat 5 / **-5**	Use **5b**	instead of 5	**5b**
	augmented / **+**	Use **5#**	instead of 5	**5#**
Root	Dominant 7th / **7**	Add **7b** note	2 notes below Root	**7b**

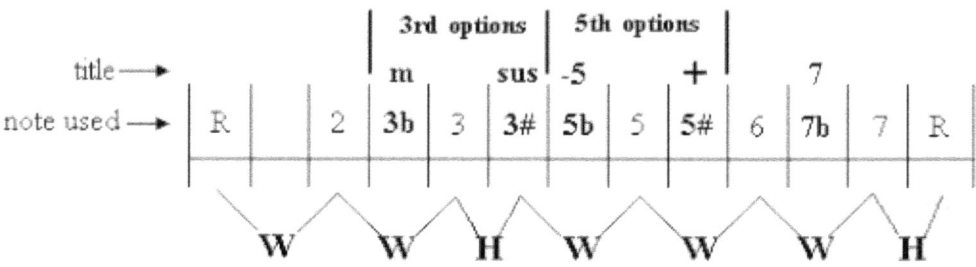

Figure 39

Now, put some of this into action. See the next page.

To make a **Cm7-5** (C minor 7 flat 5) chord, start with a C chord shown in Figure 40.

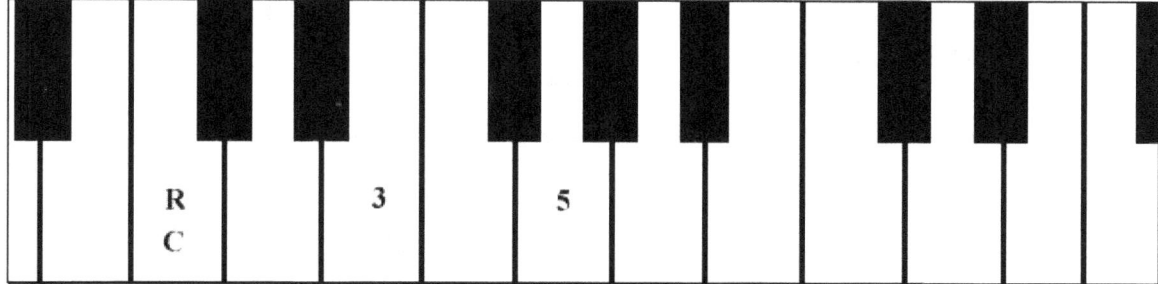
Figure 40

By **substituting 3b for the 3rd**, you get **minor**. Figure 41 shows **Cm**.

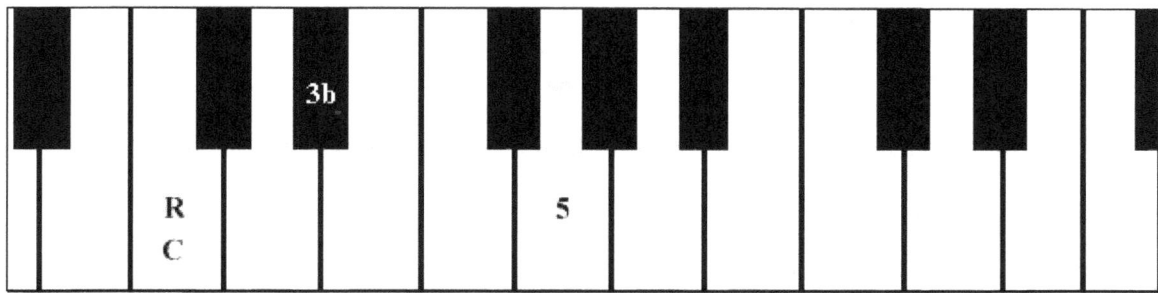
Figure 41

By **adding a 7b note**, you can add the title **seventh**. If you have minor and use the seventh rule, you get **minor seventh**. Figure 42 shows **Cm7**.

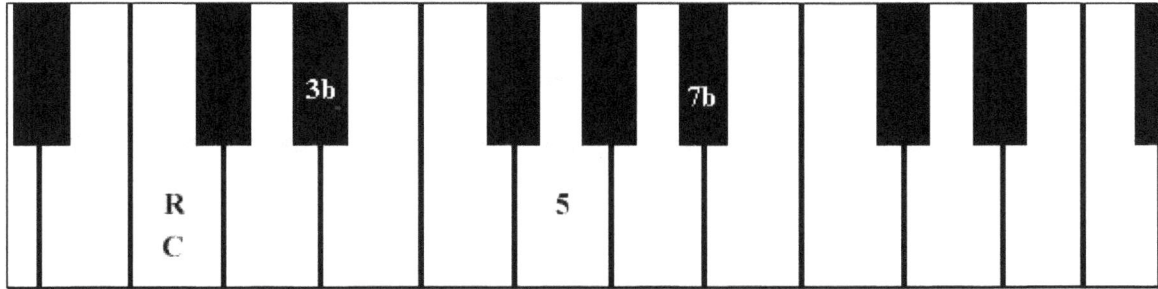
Figure 42

By substituting the 5b for the 5th, you add flat 5 (-5) to the existing title. Figure 43 shows the final chord, **Cm7-5**.

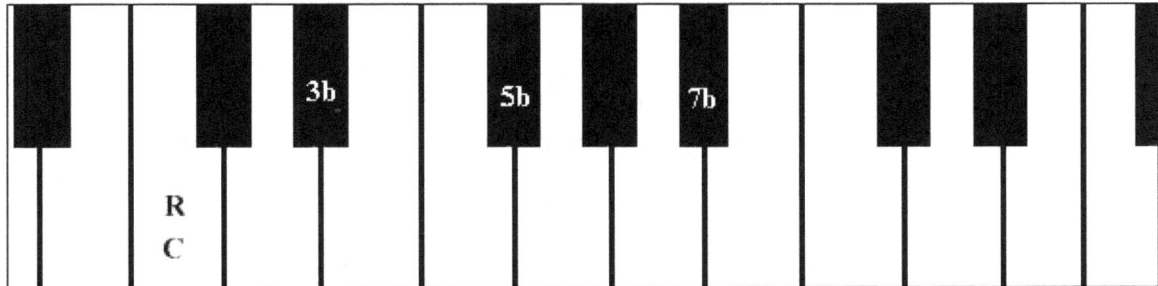
Figure 43

You READ chord titles and do as they tell you to do! Each symbol in a chord title stands for a WORD - an INSTRUCTION. READ the INSTRUCTIONS.

You are now ready to go through the Additions section.

Additions – 6th and Major 7th

You have seen how a seventh chord was made by adding the 7b scale note, to the major chord. This is an example of making a chord by ADDING a note to an existing chord. The two other examples of making chords by ADDING notes are **6th** chords (like G6) and **MAJOR 7th** chords, like **GM7**. (Please notice that the major seventh notation is a **capital M**, and not a lower case "m".[1]) Each of these can be done within ANY chord that does not already have "6", "7", or "M7" in the title. For example, you can take a Gm chord, and make it into Gm7 by ADDING the 7b note. Likewise, you can take a Gm chord and make it into a Gm6, by **adding the 6th scale note** to it. In each case, you **ADD ONE NOTE to the existing chord**. So for the title **M7**, you just **add the 7 note**. But where are these notes, in the major scale?

Looking at Figure 44, below, you can see that the **7** note is **one note below the Root**, the **7b** note is **two notes below the Root**, and the **6** note is **three notes below the Root**. Notice the grouping of the "Root options" in Figure 44.

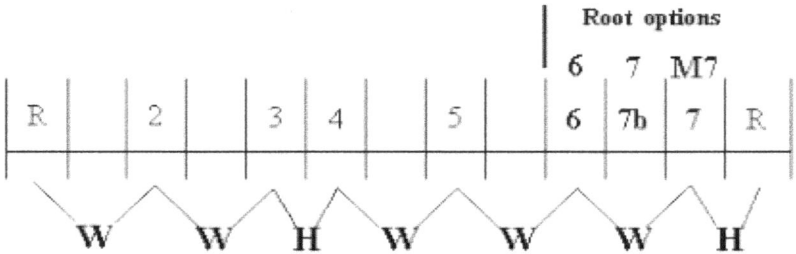

Figure 44

The MAJOR chord is made up of three kinds of notes, Roots, 3^{rds}, and 5^{ths}. If you say that the 3rd has the options "minor" and "suspended" and the 5th has the options "flat 5" and "augmented", then it is **easy to remember** that the Root has options for "Major 7th", "7th", and "6th". There is such a thing as "Interval Study" which can be very useful. As a matter of fact, you have already been using it. It is the study of how far it is, from one scale note to another. You can learn how far it is from the 3rd to the 7b, but you **don't need to know that**. So, yes, the 7b note is three notes above the 5th, but keeping the notes in the categories already given, **keeps memorization down** and makes things easier. If you NEEDED to know how far it is from the 3rd to the 7b, it would be shown and discussed. It's

---

[1] Sometimes the Major 7th title on a chord name is a "delta" character, a small triangle, like GΔ7.

NOT. Again, with the 3rd and the 5th, the options are **substitutions** to the existing 3rd and 5th scale notes, but the Root options (M7, 7, and 6) are additions of one note to the chord. Major 7th is most often shown as Δ7, like GΔ7.

Just like you added a 7b note to the Cm chord to get Cm7, in Figure 42, you could have added a 6th scale note and gotten Cm6. Then by adding the 5b, you would have ended up with a Cm6-5 instead of a Cm7-5.

So what notes are in a C suspended 6th augmented (Csus6+) chord? Starting with Root, 3rd, and 5th, you would **sharp the 3rd** for suspended (sus), **add the 6th** note for the title "6", and **sharp the 5th** for the "aug" part of the title and you're finished. You **substituted** the #3 for the 3 and the 5# for the 5, and you added the 6. It's really that easy. Where are the notes? 3# is up one note from the 3rd, 5# is up one note from the 5th, and the 6th note is three notes below any Root (preferably the one immediately above the major chord). You can do that quickly and easily. One more thing, the 5th degree titles usually go at the end of the chord name. It's just usually notated that way. Let's look at the grouping now.

ALWAYS START WITH MAJOR = R, 3, 5

3	minor / **m**	Use **3b**	instead of 3	**3b**
	suspended / **sus**	Use **3#** (4)	instead of 3	**3#**
5	flat 5 / **-5**	Use **5b**	instead of 5	**5b**
	augmented / **+**	Use **5#**	instead of 5	**5#**
R	Major 7th / Δ7	Add **7** note	1 note below R	**7**
	Dominant 7th / 7	Add **7b** note	2 notes below R	**7b**
	sixth / 6	Add **6** note	3 notes below R	**6**

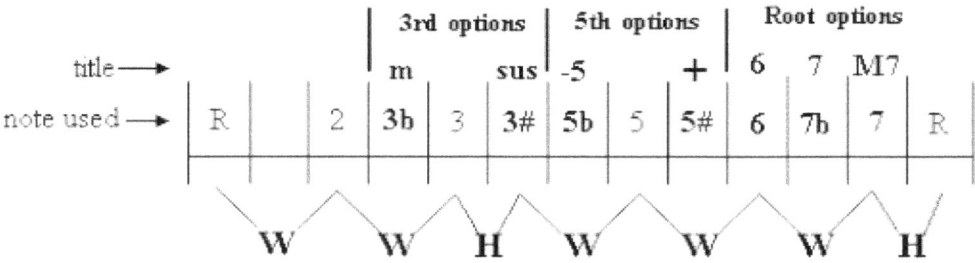

Figure 45

Are you ready for more? Next, you will be shown **combination** titles. These chord titles are single instructions that mean to **add** more than one note to a chord. You've seen them in books and sheet music. They are chords like C9 or C13. So far, every individual title you have been shown has been a single instruction. Minor means use 3b instead of the 3rd. There are titles that tell you to do more than one thing.

Combination Titles

These titles refer to "second octave" scale notes. An octave is the notes from one end of any major scale to the other end. We have been calling the starting and ending notes the Root, which is correct and proper to do, but you need to consider, now, that the Root can be the 1st and the 8th scale notes. Look below at Figure 46.

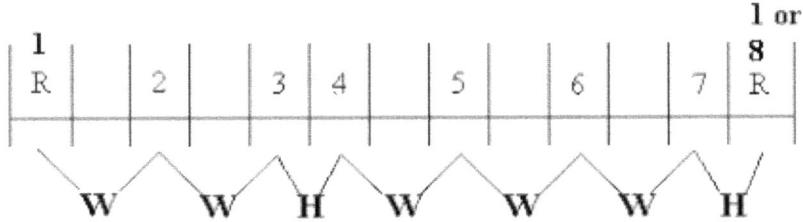

Figure 46

The scale can repeat from either Root in both directions. However, if you go into the "second octave," the scale numbers CAN be called 9, 10, etc.

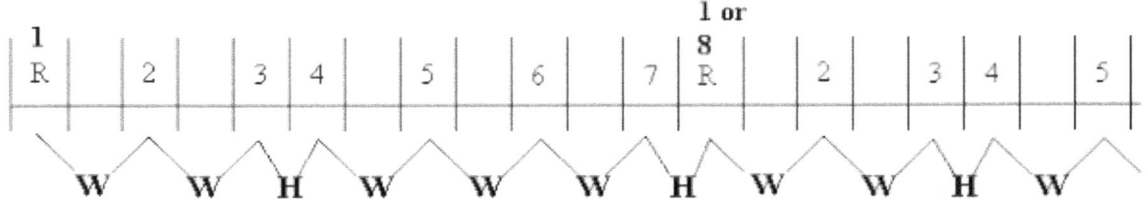

Figure 47

The numbers past 8 are still using major scale notes.

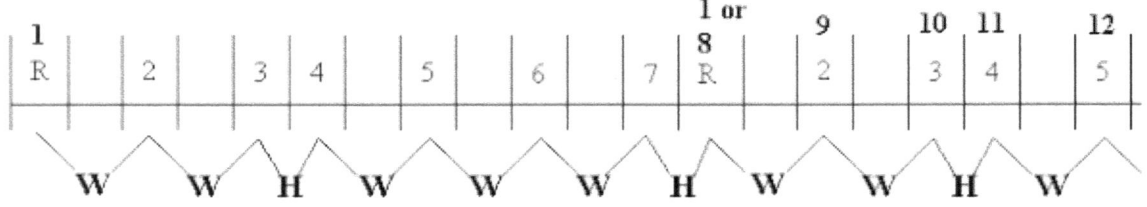

Figure 48

Now look at Figure 49. You'll see that the 10 and 12 notes are missing! The 3rd is the most important harmony to the Root. It is SO IMPORTANT that it is called the MAJOR 3rd. In ANY octave, it is the 3rd and **NOT** the 10th. The 5th is the second most important harmony to the Root. It is called the DOMINANT 5TH. In ANY octave, it is called the 5th and **NOT** the 12th.

Figure 49

If you see 9 in a chord title, like C9, the 9 in the title is telling you to **ADD** a **COMBINATION** of notes. The name of the chord is "C dominant ninth", but just like with the seventh chord, you can leave off the word "dominant" and call it "C ninth". There are two groups of COMBINATION titles. They are the "DOMINANT" group and the "MAJOR" group. Remember in the Root category, you had Δ7, 7th, and 6th. The "Δ7" was the "MAJOR seventh" and the "7" was the "DOMINANT seventh"

The title "Δ7" tells you to ADD the 7 note and the title "7" tells you to ADD the 7b note. The title "**9**" tells you to **ADD the 7b note AND the 9 note**, thus being a **COMBINATION TITLE**.

The DOMINANT group is determined by the **7b scale note**, so the ninth chord (or Dominant 9th) will have the **9 note AND the 7b note**.

The **MAJOR** group is determined by the **7 scale note**, so a **Major ninth**, shown like "Δ9", will have the **7 note and the 9 note**. It is easier to see it.

Title	Dominant	Title	Major
7	R, 3, 5, **7b**	Δ7	R, 3, 5, **7**
9	R, 3, 5, **7b, 9**	Δ9	R, 3, 5, **7, 9**

You can still use 3rd and 5th options. You can make a "minor ninth" by using the 3b instead of the 3rd, in the 9th chord. You can even do a "minor major 9th" if you use the 3b instead of the 3rd, in the Δ9 chord. Minor refers to the 3rd "degree" of the scale and "Δ9" refers to the 7 and 9 notes in combination.

The COMBINATION titles use notes moving in ODD NUMBERS and are easily distinguished by the **7b** note or the **7** note. If you say "1" instead of "Root", the Major 7th chord will become "1,3,5,**7**". The seventh chord will be "1,3,5,**7b**". Major 9 will be "1,3,5,**7,9**". Ninth will be "1,3,5,**7b,9**". Keeping this in mind, you can also have 11th, Major 11th, 13th, and Major 13th chords.

The numbers shown in parentheses below are OPTIONAL. If you DO include them, the ODD NUMBER method stays true.

Title	Dominant Group Notes	Title	Major Group Notes
7	R, 3, 5, **7b**	Δ7	R, 3, 5, **7**
9	R, 3, 5, **7b, 9**	Δ9	R, 3, 5, **7, 9**
11	R, 3, 5, **7b**, (9), **11**	Δ11	R, 3, 5, **7**, (9), **11**
13	R, 3, 5, **7b**, (9), (11), **13**	Δ13	R, 3, 5, **7**, (9), (11), **13**

How do you remember which ones are optional? The **7b or 7** for the GROUP and the **title note** itself are REQUIRED. The others are optional.

Let's try a couple of chords.

How about an easy "jazz" chord, D9? You make your D major chord and add the 7b and 9 notes to it. That's it. Remember, 9 is just two notes above a Root, most often in the second octave.

How about Abm13? Start with an Ab major chord. That should be easy enough. Find an Ab note (one note below an A note), count up four notes, and then count up three more and you have it. Now, look at the title. All the instructions are there. First make it minor by lowering the middle note, which is using the 3b instead of the 3, for minor. Next, consider the notes needed for 13th. Since it said 13 and not Δ13, it is a Dominant 13th and is in the Dominant group. So you will need the **7b**, 9, 11, and **13** notes, with the 9 and 11 being optional. Do you remember where those notes are? The 9 is 2 notes above a Root, the 11 is the same as a 3#, but usually it is in the next octave, the 13 is the same as a 6, but again it is usually in the next octave. If these notes are not played in the next octave, you might want to see the note below about optional notes before you make a decision on how you want to play the chord.

A few more words about OPTIONAL notes:

If you look the scale set-up in Figure 49, you will see that the 11th scale note is one note above the 3rd. If you include both notes, side by side, in an 11th chord or in a Major 11th chord, you will get some "dissonance" which you may not want. Dissonance is the opposite of HARMONY, so you CAN leave out the 3rd, since you MUST include the title note, the 11th. Or you could just be sure to play the 11th note that is in the "Second Octave".

In any extended chord (chords with more than three notes) you can see possibilities where notes end up close to others. Consider the Major ninth chord (R,3,5,7,9). Looking again at Figure 49, you can see that the 7 note can be beside a Root note, and the 9 note can be between a Root and a 3rd. This could give you 7,R,9,3,5. Try it, and see if it might be the sound you want. It might be perfect for some songs.

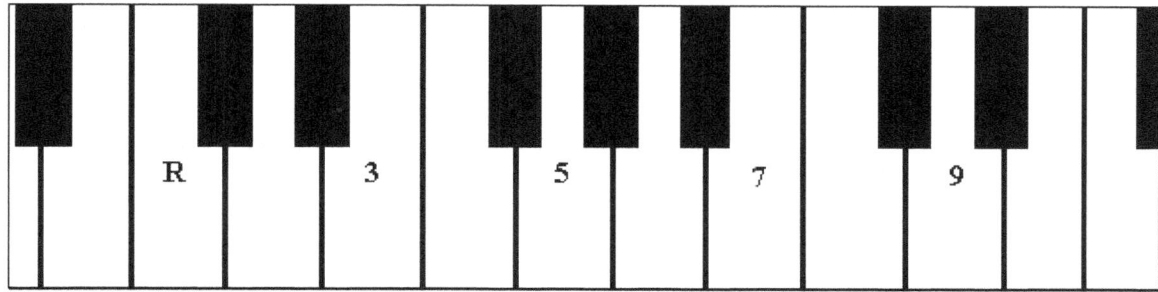

Figure 50

Here is C∆9 (C Major ninth) with "second octave" notes IN the second octave.

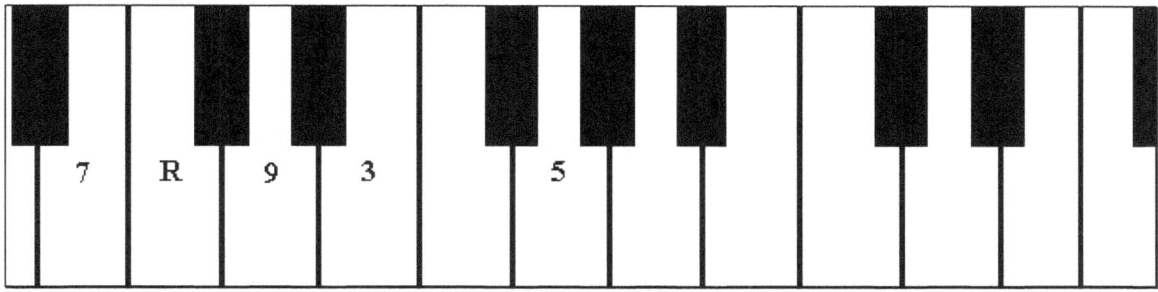

Figure 51

Here is C∆9 (C Major ninth) with "second octave" notes NOT in the second octave. Try them both and see what the difference is in the sound.

Diminished and Half-Diminished

There are two more combination titles to mention. Not only are they titles that tell you a combination of instructions, they also can have more than one name. These chords are called the HALF DIMINISHED chord and the DIMINISHED SEVENTH chord. Figure 52 is shown here so that you can see the regular scale notes and second octave notes again.

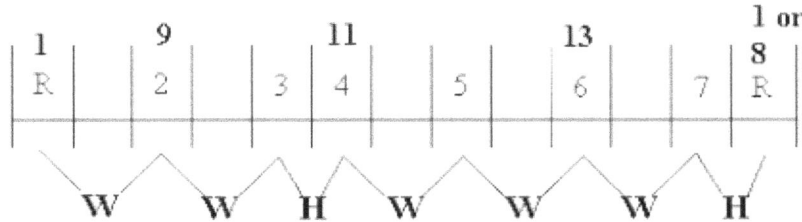

Figure 52

To diminish something is to make it lesser. If you take a major chord (R,3,5), and lower the sound of the 3rd and 5th each one note (R,3b,5b), you have a DIMINISHED chord. Another name for it could be "minor flat5" (3b gives minor, 5b gives flat5). Quite often it is not called DIMINISHED, but instead it is referred to as the HALF DIMINISHED chord. So why call it HALF diminished? This is because the DIMINISHED 7TH chord is most often called just the DIMINISHED chord. So, somehow the name HALF DIMINISHED came to be used and accepted by many musicians.

The DIMINISHED 7th chord is made by taking a 7th chord (a Dominant 7th chord, having the notes R,3,5,7b) and lowering everything except the Root. This will give you R,3b,5b,7bb (double flatted 7th). They can call this a FULL diminished chord, but usually it is referred to as just the diminished chord. The previous one is only a "HALF" diminished chord.

The 7bb note (double-flatted 7th note) is actually a 6th note. Look again at Figure 52. So, you could call the diminished seventh chord a "minor 6th flat5" chord. The names diminished and half diminished refer to how the chords were derived. Remembering that the major, minor, and seventh chords are the most used chords in music, if you take a 7th chord and flat all but the Root, it is called the diminished chord. Take the major chord and flat all but the Root and it is called the half diminished chord.

diminished (7th) / ° = R, 3b, 5b, 7bb
Like G°, called G diminished

and

half-diminished / Ø = R, 3b, 5b
Like GØ, called G half-diminished

Added Notes

The highlighted titles at the bottom of Figure 53 are usually used IN ADDITION to completed chord names. C7-9 would mean to add the flatted 9th note to a C7 chord. If you read Cm13b, it would mean to add a 13b to a C minor chord. This could also be shown "Cm add 13b". The word "add" can be also used for natural "second octave" notes. Dadd9 means to add the 9 note without also adding the 7 or the 7b. You could have "add 9" or "add 11" to tell the player to NOT include the 7 or 7b. So, all of the "second octave" notes with #'s or b's and those preceded by the word "add" are NOT to be considered combination titles. They are the exceptions and you say "add" when you use them or you just put them at the end of the chord title.

Notice that there is no 11b note or title shown. 11b would be the 3rd, and it is ALWAYS the 3rd and never anything else.

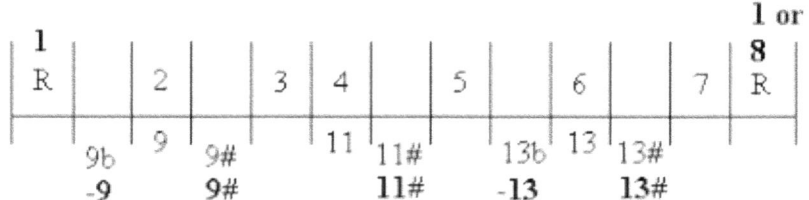

Figure 53

Also, you would never say "add 13" because the 13th note is the 6th note. Remember that if you add a 6th note (without also adding a 7 or 7b note) to any chord, you simply put a 6 in the title of the chord. So there is no "add 13" title ever used.

Before we move on, let's recap a little.

The combination chords just move in odd numbers using either the 7 or the 7b note, depending on whether the title has the Δ (or the M) before the number. These are like B7 versus BΔ7 (which can be BM7), and B9 versus BΔ9 (BM9), B11 versus BΔ11 (BM11) and so on. The 9, 11, and 13 notes are the same as the 2, 4 (or 3#) and 6 notes. Diminished chords flat everything but the root (half-dim = R,3b,5b and dim 7th = R,3b,5b, 7bb). The word "add" means to ignore the odd-numbered sequence combinations and add the named note. That's about it. But it gives you literally hundreds of possible chords you can make and use. Now, to make playing easier, let's look at chord inversions.

Inversions

Chord INVERSIONS are actually very easy to cover. The actual mechanics of them and the memorization of their results can take quite a bit of time. You will find that using inversions can not only make playing easier, but inversions can also make a sequence of chords sound BETTER.

Starting with MAJOR, which you have been making by playing the Root, 3rd, and 5th, you can now make the first inversion by playing the chord as 3rd, 5th, and Root. The first "degree" of the chord has been moved from the lowest note in the chord to the highest note. If the chord has only THREE kinds of notes in it, there will be TWO possible INVERSIONS. Again using major, the first of these inversions is to move the Root to the top, giving you 3rd, 5th, and Root. The second inversion would move the note that is NOW the lowest (the 3rd) to the top, giving you 5th, Root, and 3rd. If you now move the lowest note to the top, you will have Root, 3rd, and 5th again, which is NOT an inversion at all, so **three note chords have two inversions**.

Root	3rd	5th				major
	3rd	5th	Root			1st **inversion**
		5th	Root	3rd		2nd **inversion**
			Root	3rd	5th	major again, not an inversion.

The following diagrams (Figures 54 through 58) show how using inversions can make it easier to change from one chord to another.

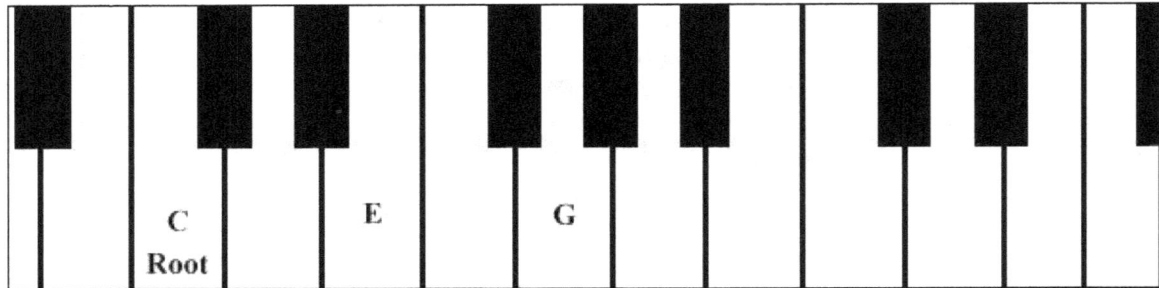

Figure 54

Above is a C chord again. Below is an F chord. Look how far you must move to get from one to the other.

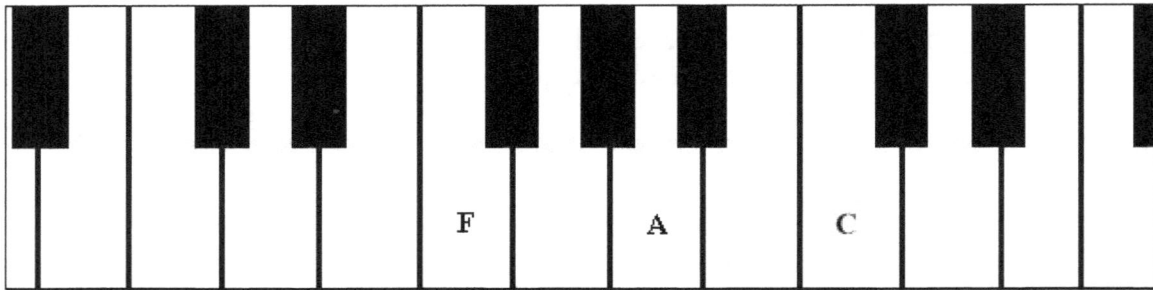

Figure 55

As you can see, you would need to move up the keyboard and that takes time. It also would have both chords "voiced" the same way. Blending of sounds, resolution, and homogeneous sounds are all things you may want to achieve, not to mention moving less from one chord to another. Look at the next page for how inversions can help you.

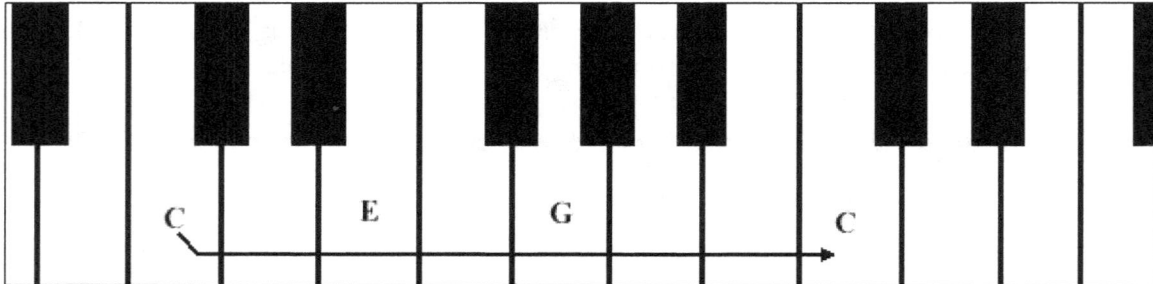

Figure 56

As said before, to make the first inversion of a chord, make the chord, then move the Root note up an octave, to the Root above the 5th note. It is shown on the next page.

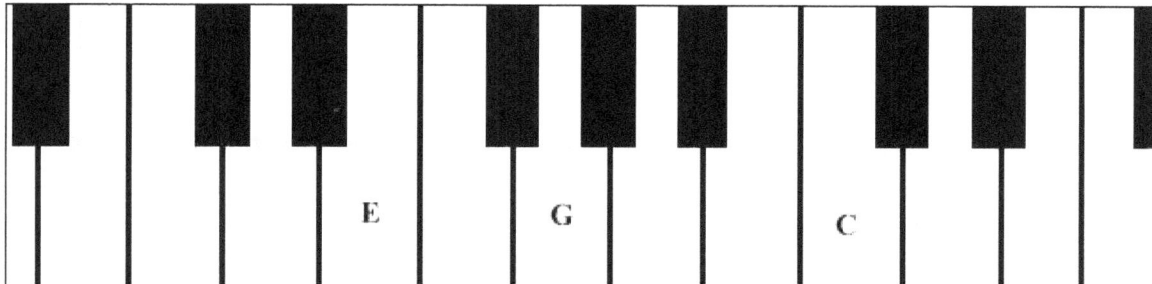

Figure 57

And here is the F chord again, below.

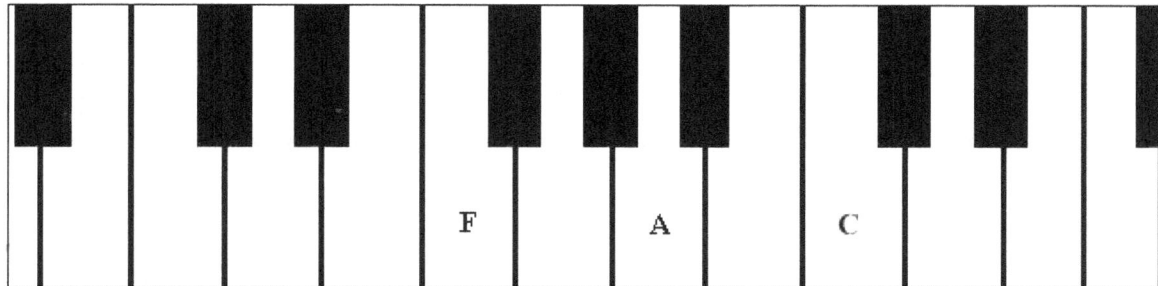

Figure 58

Look at the two keyboards immediately above and now notice how far it is from C to F using the 1st inversion of C. One note even STAYS where it is! If you play C to F the first way and then this way, you will hear a difference. The choice of whether or not to use inversions is yours to make. Most keyboard players DO use them. The Seventh chord uses four notes, Root, 3rd, 5th, and 7b. So it will have THREE inversions possible.

Root	3rd	5th	7b				major
	3rd	5th	7b	Root			**1st inversion**
		5th	7b	Root	3rd		**2nd inversion**
			7b	Root	3rd	5th	**3rd inversion**
				Root	3rd	5th	7b	(not an inversion)

You just move the lowest not to the highest position. That's pretty easy to talk about.

Yes then, inversions are easy to talk about. The hard part is up to you. The most important thing, still, is that YOU CAN MAKE the non-inverted form of ANY chord. You can then invert it, if you feel it would sound better or be easier to play the other chords before and after it. You really should experiment and see what inversions can do for you.

A chord title which MAY indicate an inversion is the slash "/". The title to the left of the slash is the chord name. To the right will be a specific Bass note to be used. **A7/G** would mean to play an A7 chord, and a G note with the left hand. The chord played with the right hand does NOT have to be an inversion of the A7 chord.

So, it looks like you are very near the end of your journey. However, you should also know that there are many ambiguities when it comes to naming chords. Here are a couple that might cause you some confusion. The Dsus chord (D suspended chord) uses the Root, the 3# (or 4), and the 5th. The sus part of the title tells you to raise the 3rd scale note. Now if you see the title Dsus4, do you raise the 4th scale note? No, this title is like saying "ATM machine." That is really saying Automated Teller Machine machine. It is a redundancy that has been accepted for some reason. Dsus4 means use the 3# note, which we know is the 4th scale note. The title Dsus2 does not mean to sharp the 2nd scale note. That would raise it to the 3b note, the note used for minor. Dsus2 means to add the 2nd scale note. Since the 2nd scale note can be called the 9th scale note, it is preferable to not use the "sus2" title, but the "add9" title, instead.

One of the most valuable parts of this manual on understanding chords will be the Review Page. You should come back to it often. The pages that follow the Review Page list the chords you can make when you have made it to this point. Good luck with your musical endeavors, whatever they may be.

Chapter 5 The CHORDMASTER REVIEW PAGES

ALWAYS START WITH MAJOR = R, 3, 5

Note	Title / Symbol			
3	minor / **m**	Use **3b**	instead of 3	**3b**
	suspended / **sus**	Use **3#** (4)	instead of 3	**3#**
5	flat 5 / **-5**	Use **5b**	instead of 5	**5b**
	augmented / **+**	Use **5#**	instead of 5	**5#**
R	Major 7th / Δ7	Add **7** note	1 note below R	**7**
	Dominant 7th / **7**	Add **7b** note	2 notes below R	**7b**
	sixth / **6**	Add **6** note	3 notes below R	**6**

Title	Dominant	Title	Major
7	R, 3, 5, **7b**	Δ7	R, 3, 5, **7**
9	R, 3, 5, 7b, **9**	Δ9	R, 3, 5, 7, **9**
11	R, 3, 5, 7b, (9), **11**	Δ11	R, 3, 5, 7, (9), **11**
13	R, 3, 5, 7b, (9), (11), **13**	Δ13	R, 3, 5, 7, (9), (11), **13**

3rd and 5th substitutions can also be made to any of the above.
Just be sure to include the corresponding title (like m or -5).

diminished (7th) / ° = **R, 3b, 5b, 7bb**   half-diminished / Ø = **R, 3b. 5b**

add - add the specified single note

Be sure to see the next pages for the list of chords.

CHORDMASTER CHORD LIST
Over 1,082 Chords <u>You</u> <u>Can</u> <u>Make</u> <u>NOW!</u>

The following list of chords has a "running total" under each section. The sections are not "families" of chords. They are just the groupings of possible chords you can make with the knowledge of the previous group, following the initial 12 major chords. If you see any chords you think you cannot make, go back and review the chapter for those titles. You should be able to make <u>all</u> the chords listed below. Remember that since there are 12 notes, you can make 12 of every chord title listed. That is why there is a "12" beside each title.

12 major
  12

12 minor
12 suspended
  36

12 aug
12 -5
  60

12 m aug
12 m -5
12 sus aug
12 sus -5
  108

12 6th
12 m6
12 sus6
12 6aug
12 6-5
12 m6aug
12 sus6aug
12 m6-5
12 sus6-5
  216

12 seventh
12 m7
12 sus7
12 7aug
12 7-5
12 m7aug
12 sus7aug
12 m7-5
12 sus7-5
324

12 Δ7
12 mΔ7
12 susΔ7
12 Δ7aug
12 Δ7-5
12 mΔ7aug
12 susΔ7aug
12 mΔ7-5
12 mΔ7-5
432

12 ninth
12 m9
12 sus9
12 9aug
12 9-5
12 m9aug
12 sus9aug
12 m9-5
12 sus9-5
540

12 Δ9
12 mΔ9
12 susΔ9
12 Δ9aug
12 Δ9-5
12 mΔ9aug
12 susΔ9aug
12 mΔ9-5

12 mΔ9-5
648

12 eleventh
12 m11
12 sus11
12 11aug
12 11-5
12 m11aug
12 sus11aug
12 m11-5
12 sus11-5
756

12 Δ11
12 mΔ11
12 susΔ11
12 Δ11aug
12 Δ11-5
12 mΔ11aug
12 susΔ11aug
12 mΔ11-5
12 mΔ11-5
864

12 thirteenth
12 m13
12 sus13
12 13aug
12 13-5
12 m13aug
12 sus13aug
12 m13-5
12 sus13-5
972

12 Δ13
12 mΔ13
12 susΔ13
12 Δ13aug
12 Δ13-5

12 mΔ13aug
12 susΔ13aug
12 mΔ13-5
12 mΔ13-5
   1,080

12 diminished
12 half diminished
   1,082

Then there are chords like Cm add 13b and D add 9 **and how many others?**

OVER 5,592 POSSIBLE CHORDS!

Now add all of the **Inversions!!** Remember, any four note chord like a 7th chord has three possible inversions. Now consider a 13th chord. It has 6 inversions possible. Let's see…

108 three note chords with two inversions for each = 324 chords

324 four note chords with three inversions each = 1296 chords

216 five note chords with four inversions each = 1080 chords

216 six note chords with five inversions each = 1296 chords

216 seven note chords with six inversions each = 1512 chords

12 half-diminished chords with two inversions each = 36 chords

12 diminished seventh chords with three inversions each = 48 chords

TOTAL   -   5,592 chords!

PLUS all the chords that add single notes (like Dadd9) and their inversions. Now you can't be expected to know all the chords by heart, with all the inversions, but you have been provided the knowledge to make well over 5,592 chords!

How **MUCH YOU KNOW!**

HAVE FUN AND COME BACK OFTEN

Index

+

+. *See* AUGMENTED

Δ

Δ7. *See* Major 7th

5

-5. *See* flat 5

6

6th. *See* SIXTH

7

7bb note
    This is a 6th, so why 7bb?. *See* DIMINISHED SEVENTH
7th. *See* SEVENTH

A

A7/G
    Example of a chord with a specified bass note, 4-19
Abm13
    Create an Abm13 chord, 4-14
alphabetically
    The way notes move, 1-2
AUGMENTED
    Definition of the augmented chord title, 4-7

B

basics, 4-8

C

C suspended 6th augmented
    How to create a Csus6+ chord, 4-11
C7-9
    Definition of a C7-9 chord, 4-16
Chords
    Definition of a chord, 1-3
CM9
    Picture of a CM9 chord, 4-15

D

D major scale, 2-2
D9
    Create a D9 chord, 4-14

DIMINISHED SEVENTH
    Definition of diminished 7th chords, 4-15
dissonance, 4-14
dominant 7th
    What is the Dominant 7th?, 4-4

E

E major scale, 2-4
extended chord
    Definition of extended chords, 4-15

F

Figure 1
    The standard view of a keyboard, 1-1
Figure 14
    The set-up for the E major scale, 2-4
Figure 2
    A better view of the keyboard, 1-2
Figure 20
    Chart of Natural Major Scales, 2-6
Figure 21. *See* Figure 2
Figure 22
    Picture of a C major chord, 3-2
Figure 23
    Picture of a G major chord, 3-2
Figure 24
    Picture of a Gb major chord, 3-3
Figure 25
    Picture of an E major chord, 3-3
Figure 26
    Locating the 3b scale note, 4-2
Figure 28
    Picture of a Cm chord, 4-2
Figure 29
    Picture of an E major chord, 4-3
Figure 3
    Chart of notes, 1-2
Figure 30
    Picture of an Em chord, 4-3
Figure 31
    Locating the 7b scale note, 4-3
Figure 34
    Picture of a C7 chord, 4-4
Figure 36
    Picture of a D7 chord, 4-5
Figure 37
    View of 3rd scale note options, 4-6
Figure 38
    View of 5th scale note options, 4-7
Figure 39
    View of options for the basics, 4-8
Figure 4
    The C Major Scale, 2-1
Figure 42
    Picture of a Cm7 chord, 4-9
Figure 43

Picture of a Cm7-5 chord, 4-9
Figure 44
    View of Root Options, 4-10
Figure 45
    View of all First-Octave options, 4-11
Figure 47
    View of Second-Octave concept, 4-12
Figure 48
    View of Second-Octave notes, 4-12
Figure 49
    View of Entire Second-Octave, 4-13
Figure 5
    The set-up for major scales, 2-2
Figure 51
    Picture of a CM9 chord, condensed, 4-15
Figure 52
    View of Second Octave notes with titles, 4-16
Figure 55
    Creating a 1st inversion of a C chord, 4-18
Figure 56
    Finished 1st inversion of a C chord, 4-19
Figure 6
    Set-up for the D major scale, 2-2
First Test
    Your First Test, 1-4
five rules, so far, 4-8
flat 5
    Definition of flat 5 chord title, 4-7
FLAT notes, 1-1

H

HALF DIMINISHED
    Definition of half-diminished chords, 4-15
Half step
    Definition of a half step, 2-1
How many notes exist?, 1-1

M

M7. *See* Major 7th
Major 7th
    Definition of a Major 7th chord, 4-10
major scale
    Definition of a major scale, 2-1
MINOR
    The true definition of minor, 4-2
Minor Chords, 4-1
minor seventh, 4-6

N

NATURAL major scales
    To View, 2-6
NATURAL notes, 1-1
note
    Definition of a note. *See tone*
    Definition of a note or tone, 1-1

O

order of the notes, 1-2

R

ROOT, 2-4
Root note, the 3rd note, and the 5th note
    Definition of a major chord, 2-7

S

Second Test, 2-8
Seventh chords
    Definition of a 7th chord, 4-3
SHARP notes, 1-1
SIXTH
    Definition of a sixth chord, 4-10
sus. *See SUSPENDED*
SUSPENDED
    Definition of Suspended, 4-6

T

The Secret to Music Theory, 2-7
tone
    Definition. *See* note

U

up in sound, 1-2

W

Whole step
    Definition of a whole step, 2-1

Y

Your LAST Test, 3-5

NOTES

This is where you can jot down your own thoughts and ideas.

www.ingramcontent.com/pod-product-compliance
Lightning Source LLC
Chambersburg PA
CBHW080528110426
42742CB00017B/3269